MERMAIDS

SELINA  FENECH

Includes 2 each of 25 mermaid coloring images by Selina Fenech.

See how the colors the artist chose for her paintings at
www.selinafenech.com

Mermaids - Calm Ocean Coloring Collection
by Selina Fenech
First Published May 2015
Published by Fairies and Fantasy PTY LTD
ISBN: 978-0-9943554-0-9

www.selinafenech.com

Printed in Great Britain
by Amazon.co.uk, Ltd.,
Marston Gate.